50 Healthy Dinner Recipes for Life

By: Kelly Johnson

Table of Contents

- Grilled Lemon Herb Chicken
- Quinoa-Stuffed Bell Peppers
- Baked Salmon with Avocado Salsa
- Zucchini Noodles with Pesto
- Grilled Tofu and Veggie Skewers
- Cauliflower Fried Rice
- Chicken and Sweet Potato Sheet Pan Dinner
- Shrimp and Broccoli Stir-Fry
- Chickpea and Spinach Curry
- Avocado Chicken Salad
- Turkey Meatballs with Zucchini Noodles
- Spaghetti Squash Primavera
- Spicy Chickpea Tacos
- Grilled Veggie and Hummus Wraps
- Lemon Garlic Roasted Chicken Thighs
- Sweet Potato and Black Bean Chili
- Cauliflower and Chickpea Buddha Bowl
- Grilled Salmon with Mango Salsa
- Veggie-Packed Lentil Soup
- Stuffed Acorn Squash with Quinoa
- Asian-Inspired Chicken Lettuce Wraps
- Sweet Potato and Kale Frittata
- Baked Chicken Parmesan with Zoodles
- Veggie and Hummus Stuffed Pita
- Spicy Black Bean and Avocado Salad
- Roasted Brussels Sprouts and Sweet Potato
- Turkey and Spinach Meatloaf
- Quinoa Salad with Roasted Vegetables
- Garlic Parmesan Roasted Shrimp
- Broccoli and Cheddar Stuffed Chicken Breast
- Grilled Chicken with Greek Salad
- Avocado and Tuna Salad Lettuce Wraps
- Roasted Vegetables with Tahini Dressing
- Coconut Curry Chicken and Veggies
- Blackened Salmon with Quinoa

- Roasted Cauliflower with Tahini
- Sweet Potato and Spinach Gratin
- Grilled Portobello Mushrooms with Feta
- Miso Glazed Chicken with Veggies
- Tempeh and Vegetable Stir-Fry
- Greek Chicken Souvlaki Bowls
- Roasted Eggplant with Tomato Sauce
- Zucchini and Carrot Fritters
- Grilled Cod with Cucumber Salad
- Tofu and Broccoli Stir-Fry
- Coconut Lime Chicken with Rice
- Beetroot Salad with Walnuts
- Mediterranean Chickpea Salad
- Quinoa and Black Bean Stuffed Peppers
- Grilled Veggie and Quinoa Bowl

Grilled Lemon Herb Chicken

Ingredients:

- 4 boneless, skinless chicken breasts
- 2 tablespoons olive oil
- 2 lemons (zested and juiced)
- 4 garlic cloves, minced
- 1 tablespoon fresh thyme, chopped (or 1 teaspoon dried thyme)
- 1 tablespoon fresh rosemary, chopped (or 1 teaspoon dried rosemary)
- 1 teaspoon dried oregano
- Salt and pepper to taste

Instructions:

1. **Prepare the marinade**: In a medium bowl, whisk together olive oil, lemon juice, lemon zest, minced garlic, thyme, rosemary, oregano, salt, and pepper until fully combined.
2. **Marinate the chicken**: Place the chicken breasts in a resealable plastic bag or shallow dish. Pour the marinade over the chicken, ensuring it is evenly coated. Seal the bag or cover the dish and refrigerate for at least 30 minutes (up to 2 hours for best flavor).
3. **Preheat the grill**: Preheat your grill or grill pan to medium-high heat. Make sure the grill grates are lightly oiled to prevent sticking.
4. **Grill the chicken**: Remove the chicken from the marinade and discard the leftover marinade. Place the chicken breasts on the hot grill. Cook for 6-7 minutes per side, or until the chicken reaches an internal temperature of 165°F (75°C) and has nice grill marks.
5. **Serve**: Let the chicken rest for 5 minutes before slicing. Serve with your favorite side dishes, such as grilled vegetables, rice, or a fresh salad.

Quinoa-Stuffed Bell Peppers

Ingredients:

- 4 large bell peppers, tops cut off and seeds removed
- 1 cup quinoa, cooked
- 1 can black beans, drained and rinsed
- 1 cup corn kernels (fresh, frozen, or canned)
- 1 cup diced tomatoes
- 1 tablespoon olive oil
- 1 teaspoon cumin
- 1 teaspoon chili powder
- Salt and pepper to taste
- 1/2 cup shredded cheese (optional)

Instructions:

1. Preheat the oven to 375°F (190°C).
2. In a large bowl, mix cooked quinoa, black beans, corn, diced tomatoes, olive oil, cumin, chili powder, salt, and pepper.
3. Stuff each bell pepper with the quinoa mixture and place in a baking dish.
4. Cover with foil and bake for 25-30 minutes.
5. If using cheese, remove foil and sprinkle cheese on top of the stuffed peppers, then bake uncovered for an additional 5-10 minutes until cheese is melted and peppers are tender.

Baked Salmon with Avocado Salsa

Ingredients:

- 4 salmon fillets
- 2 tablespoons olive oil
- 1 tablespoon lemon juice
- 1 teaspoon garlic powder
- Salt and pepper to taste
- 2 ripe avocados, diced
- 1/2 cup cherry tomatoes, diced
- 1/4 cup red onion, finely chopped
- 2 tablespoons cilantro, chopped
- 1 tablespoon lime juice

Instructions:

1. Preheat the oven to 400°F (200°C).
2. Place the salmon fillets on a baking sheet, drizzle with olive oil, lemon juice, and season with garlic powder, salt, and pepper.
3. Bake for 12-15 minutes or until salmon flakes easily with a fork.
4. In a bowl, combine avocado, tomatoes, red onion, cilantro, and lime juice. Stir gently to combine.
5. Serve the baked salmon topped with fresh avocado salsa.

Zucchini Noodles with Pesto

Ingredients:

- 2 large zucchinis, spiralized into noodles
- 1 cup fresh basil leaves
- 1/4 cup pine nuts (or walnuts)
- 2 garlic cloves
- 1/4 cup Parmesan cheese
- 1/4 cup olive oil
- Salt and pepper to taste

Instructions:

1. In a food processor, combine basil, pine nuts, garlic, Parmesan, olive oil, salt, and pepper. Blend until smooth.
2. Heat a large skillet over medium heat and sauté zucchini noodles for 2-3 minutes until slightly softened.
3. Toss the zucchini noodles with the pesto sauce until well coated and serve.

Grilled Tofu and Veggie Skewers

Ingredients:

- 1 block firm tofu, pressed and cubed
- 1 red bell pepper, chopped into chunks
- 1 zucchini, sliced
- 1 red onion, chopped into chunks
- 1 tablespoon olive oil
- 2 tablespoons soy sauce
- 1 tablespoon maple syrup
- 1 teaspoon garlic powder
- Salt and pepper to taste

Instructions:

1. Preheat the grill to medium heat.
2. In a bowl, whisk together olive oil, soy sauce, maple syrup, garlic powder, salt, and pepper.
3. Thread tofu and vegetables onto skewers.
4. Brush the skewers with the marinade and grill for 5-7 minutes on each side until veggies are tender and tofu is golden.

Cauliflower Fried Rice

Ingredients:

- 1 medium cauliflower, grated or processed into rice-sized pieces
- 2 tablespoons sesame oil
- 1 cup mixed vegetables (carrots, peas, corn, etc.)
- 2 garlic cloves, minced
- 2 eggs, lightly beaten
- 2 tablespoons soy sauce
- 1 green onion, chopped

Instructions:

1. Heat sesame oil in a large skillet or wok over medium heat. Add garlic and cook for 1 minute.
2. Add mixed vegetables and cook for 3-4 minutes until tender.
3. Push veggies to the side and scramble the eggs in the same skillet.
4. Add cauliflower rice to the pan, stir well, and cook for 5-7 minutes until cauliflower is tender.
5. Stir in soy sauce and green onions, then serve.

Chicken and Sweet Potato Sheet Pan Dinner

Ingredients:

- 4 boneless, skinless chicken breasts
- 2 large sweet potatoes, cubed
- 1 tablespoon olive oil
- 1 teaspoon paprika
- 1 teaspoon garlic powder
- 1/2 teaspoon ground cumin
- Salt and pepper to taste
- 1 tablespoon fresh parsley, chopped (for garnish)

Instructions:

1. Preheat the oven to 400°F (200°C).
2. Toss sweet potato cubes in olive oil, paprika, garlic powder, cumin, salt, and pepper. Spread evenly on a baking sheet.
3. Season chicken breasts with the same spices and place them on the baking sheet.
4. Roast for 25-30 minutes until chicken is cooked through and sweet potatoes are tender.
5. Garnish with fresh parsley and serve.

Shrimp and Broccoli Stir-Fry

Ingredients:

- 1 lb shrimp, peeled and deveined
- 2 cups broccoli florets
- 1 tablespoon sesame oil
- 2 garlic cloves, minced
- 1 tablespoon soy sauce
- 1 tablespoon honey
- 1 teaspoon grated ginger
- 1/2 tablespoon rice vinegar
- 1 tablespoon green onion, chopped

Instructions:

1. Heat sesame oil in a large skillet over medium heat.
2. Add garlic and ginger, cooking for 1-2 minutes until fragrant.
3. Add shrimp and cook for 2-3 minutes per side until pink and cooked through.
4. Add broccoli, soy sauce, honey, and rice vinegar. Stir to combine and cook for 4-5 more minutes until broccoli is tender.
5. Garnish with green onions and serve.

Chickpea and Spinach Curry

Ingredients:

- 1 can chickpeas, drained and rinsed
- 3 cups fresh spinach
- 1 can diced tomatoes
- 1 can coconut milk
- 1 tablespoon curry powder
- 1 teaspoon turmeric
- 1 teaspoon cumin
- Salt and pepper to taste
- 1 tablespoon olive oil

Instructions:

1. Heat olive oil in a large pot over medium heat. Add curry powder, turmeric, and cumin and cook for 1-2 minutes until fragrant.
2. Add chickpeas, diced tomatoes, and coconut milk. Stir to combine and simmer for 10 minutes.
3. Add fresh spinach and cook until wilted.
4. Season with salt and pepper, and serve with rice or naan.

Avocado Chicken Salad

Ingredients:

- 2 cups cooked chicken, shredded
- 2 ripe avocados, mashed
- 1/4 cup Greek yogurt
- 1 tablespoon lime juice
- 1/2 red onion, finely chopped
- 1/4 cup cilantro, chopped
- Salt and pepper to taste

Instructions:

1. In a large bowl, combine shredded chicken, mashed avocados, Greek yogurt, lime juice, red onion, and cilantro.
2. Season with salt and pepper and mix until well combined.
3. Serve on a bed of greens, in a wrap, or with crackers.

Turkey Meatballs with Zucchini Noodles

Ingredients:

- 1 lb ground turkey
- 1/2 cup breadcrumbs (or almond flour for a low-carb option)
- 1/4 cup grated Parmesan cheese
- 1 egg
- 2 garlic cloves, minced
- 1 teaspoon dried oregano
- Salt and pepper to taste
- 2 medium zucchinis, spiralized into noodles
- 1 tablespoon olive oil
- 1/2 cup marinara sauce (optional)

Instructions:

1. Preheat the oven to 375°F (190°C).
2. In a large bowl, mix ground turkey, breadcrumbs, Parmesan, egg, garlic, oregano, salt, and pepper.
3. Form the mixture into meatballs and place them on a baking sheet lined with parchment paper.
4. Bake for 20-25 minutes until cooked through.
5. While the meatballs bake, heat olive oil in a large pan over medium heat. Add zucchini noodles and sauté for 2-3 minutes until just tender.
6. Serve meatballs over zucchini noodles with marinara sauce if desired.

Spaghetti Squash Primavera

Ingredients:

- 1 medium spaghetti squash
- 1 tablespoon olive oil
- 1 cup cherry tomatoes, halved
- 1 zucchini, sliced
- 1 yellow bell pepper, diced
- 1/2 red onion, chopped
- 2 garlic cloves, minced
- 1/2 teaspoon dried basil
- Salt and pepper to taste
- 1/4 cup fresh basil, chopped
- Parmesan cheese, for garnish (optional)

Instructions:

1. Preheat the oven to 400°F (200°C).
2. Cut the spaghetti squash in half lengthwise, remove the seeds, and drizzle with olive oil. Place cut-side down on a baking sheet.
3. Roast for 40-45 minutes until tender. Use a fork to scrape out the strands.
4. In a large pan, heat olive oil over medium heat. Add garlic, tomatoes, zucchini, bell pepper, and onion. Sauté for 5-7 minutes until vegetables are tender.
5. Stir in the spaghetti squash strands, basil, salt, and pepper.
6. Garnish with fresh basil and Parmesan cheese before serving.

Spicy Chickpea Tacos

Ingredients:

- 1 can chickpeas, drained and rinsed
- 1 tablespoon olive oil
- 1 teaspoon chili powder
- 1 teaspoon cumin
- 1/2 teaspoon paprika
- 1/4 teaspoon cayenne pepper (optional for extra heat)
- Salt and pepper to taste
- 8 small corn tortillas
- 1 avocado, sliced
- 1/2 cup shredded lettuce
- 1/4 cup diced tomatoes
- 2 tablespoons fresh cilantro, chopped
- Lime wedges for serving

Instructions:

1. Preheat the oven to 400°F (200°C).
2. In a bowl, toss chickpeas with olive oil, chili powder, cumin, paprika, cayenne, salt, and pepper.
3. Spread chickpeas in a single layer on a baking sheet and bake for 20-25 minutes until crispy.
4. Warm the tortillas in a dry skillet or microwave.
5. Assemble tacos by filling each tortilla with spicy chickpeas, avocado, lettuce, tomatoes, and cilantro.
6. Serve with lime wedges for squeezing.

Grilled Veggie and Hummus Wraps

Ingredients:

- 1 zucchini, sliced
- 1 red bell pepper, sliced
- 1 red onion, sliced
- 1 tablespoon olive oil
- Salt and pepper to taste
- 4 whole wheat or spinach wraps
- 1 cup hummus
- 1/4 cup fresh parsley, chopped

Instructions:

1. Preheat the grill or grill pan to medium-high heat.
2. Toss the zucchini, bell pepper, and onion in olive oil, salt, and pepper.
3. Grill the vegetables for 3-4 minutes per side until tender and slightly charred.
4. Spread a generous amount of hummus onto each wrap.
5. Top with grilled veggies and garnish with fresh parsley.
6. Roll up the wraps and serve immediately.

Lemon Garlic Roasted Chicken Thighs

Ingredients:

- 4 bone-in, skin-on chicken thighs
- 2 tablespoons olive oil
- 4 garlic cloves, minced
- 1 tablespoon lemon zest
- 2 tablespoons lemon juice
- 1 teaspoon dried rosemary
- Salt and pepper to taste

Instructions:

1. Preheat the oven to 400°F (200°C).
2. In a small bowl, whisk together olive oil, garlic, lemon zest, lemon juice, rosemary, salt, and pepper.
3. Rub the chicken thighs with the lemon-garlic mixture and place them on a baking sheet.
4. Roast for 35-40 minutes until the chicken reaches an internal temperature of 165°F (75°C) and the skin is crispy.
5. Serve with your favorite sides, like roasted vegetables or a fresh salad.

Sweet Potato and Black Bean Chili

Ingredients:

- 2 medium sweet potatoes, peeled and diced
- 1 tablespoon olive oil
- 1 onion, chopped
- 2 garlic cloves, minced
- 1 can black beans, drained and rinsed
- 1 can diced tomatoes
- 1 teaspoon ground cumin
- 1 teaspoon chili powder
- 1/2 teaspoon smoked paprika
- Salt and pepper to taste
- 4 cups vegetable broth
- 1/2 cup fresh cilantro, chopped (for garnish)

Instructions:

1. Heat olive oil in a large pot over medium heat. Add onion and garlic, and sauté for 5 minutes until softened.
2. Add sweet potatoes, black beans, diced tomatoes, cumin, chili powder, smoked paprika, salt, and pepper. Stir to combine.
3. Pour in vegetable broth and bring to a boil.
4. Lower the heat and simmer for 25-30 minutes until sweet potatoes are tender.
5. Garnish with fresh cilantro and serve.

Cauliflower and Chickpea Buddha Bowl

Ingredients:

- 1 small cauliflower, cut into florets
- 1 can chickpeas, drained and rinsed
- 1 tablespoon olive oil
- 1 teaspoon paprika
- Salt and pepper to taste
- 1 cup cooked quinoa
- 1/2 cucumber, sliced
- 1/2 avocado, sliced
- 2 tablespoons tahini
- 1 tablespoon lemon juice
- 1 teaspoon honey

Instructions:

1. Preheat the oven to 400°F (200°C).
2. Toss cauliflower and chickpeas with olive oil, paprika, salt, and pepper. Spread on a baking sheet.
3. Roast for 25-30 minutes until cauliflower is golden and chickpeas are crispy.
4. In a bowl, combine quinoa, cucumber, avocado, cauliflower, and chickpeas.
5. In a small bowl, whisk together tahini, lemon juice, and honey. Drizzle over the bowl and serve.

Grilled Salmon with Mango Salsa

Ingredients:

- 4 salmon fillets
- 2 tablespoons olive oil
- Salt and pepper to taste
- 1 ripe mango, peeled and diced
- 1/4 red onion, finely chopped
- 1/4 cup fresh cilantro, chopped
- 1 tablespoon lime juice

Instructions:

1. Preheat the grill to medium-high heat.
2. Drizzle salmon fillets with olive oil and season with salt and pepper.
3. Grill the salmon for 4-5 minutes per side until cooked through.
4. In a bowl, combine mango, red onion, cilantro, and lime juice to make the salsa.
5. Serve the grilled salmon topped with mango salsa.

Veggie-Packed Lentil Soup

Ingredients:

- 1 cup dried lentils, rinsed
- 1 tablespoon olive oil
- 1 onion, chopped
- 2 carrots, diced
- 2 celery stalks, diced
- 2 garlic cloves, minced
- 1 can diced tomatoes
- 4 cups vegetable broth
- 1 teaspoon ground cumin
- 1/2 teaspoon turmeric
- Salt and pepper to taste
- 1/2 cup spinach, chopped (optional)

Instructions:

1. Heat olive oil in a large pot over medium heat. Add onion, carrots, celery, and garlic. Sauté for 5-7 minutes until softened.
2. Add lentils, tomatoes, vegetable broth, cumin, turmeric, salt, and pepper. Bring to a boil.
3. Lower the heat and simmer for 25-30 minutes until lentils are tender.
4. Stir in spinach (if using) and cook for another 2 minutes.
5. Serve warm.

Stuffed Acorn Squash with Quinoa

Ingredients:

- 2 acorn squashes, halved and seeds removed
- 1 tablespoon olive oil
- Salt and pepper to taste
- 1 cup cooked quinoa
- 1/2 cup dried cranberries
- 1/4 cup chopped pecans or walnuts
- 1/2 teaspoon ground cinnamon
- 1 tablespoon maple syrup

Instructions:

1. Preheat the oven to 400°F (200°C).
2. Drizzle the squash halves with olive oil and season with salt and pepper.
3. Roast the squash halves cut-side down on a baking sheet for 30-35 minutes until tender.
4. In a bowl, combine quinoa, cranberries, pecans, cinnamon, and maple syrup.
5. Fill each squash half with the quinoa mixture and serve warm.

Asian-Inspired Chicken Lettuce Wraps

Ingredients:

- 1 lb ground chicken
- 2 tablespoons soy sauce (or tamari for gluten-free)
- 1 tablespoon hoisin sauce
- 1 tablespoon rice vinegar
- 1 teaspoon sesame oil
- 2 garlic cloves, minced
- 1-inch piece fresh ginger, grated
- 1/2 cup shredded carrots
- 1/2 cup water chestnuts, chopped
- 1/4 cup green onions, chopped
- 1 tablespoon sesame seeds (optional)
- 1 head of butter lettuce, leaves separated

Instructions:

1. Heat a skillet over medium heat and cook ground chicken until browned, breaking it apart with a spoon.
2. Add garlic and ginger, and cook for another minute until fragrant.
3. Stir in soy sauce, hoisin sauce, rice vinegar, and sesame oil. Cook for 2-3 minutes.
4. Add shredded carrots, water chestnuts, and green onions, stirring to combine.
5. Remove from heat and let cool slightly.
6. Spoon the chicken mixture into lettuce leaves, garnish with sesame seeds, and serve.

Sweet Potato and Kale Frittata

Ingredients:

- 2 medium sweet potatoes, peeled and diced
- 1 tablespoon olive oil
- 1 onion, chopped
- 2 garlic cloves, minced
- 2 cups kale, chopped
- 8 large eggs
- 1/4 cup milk
- Salt and pepper to taste
- 1/4 cup feta cheese (optional)

Instructions:

1. Preheat the oven to 375°F (190°C).
2. In a large skillet, heat olive oil over medium heat. Add sweet potatoes and cook until tender, about 10-12 minutes.
3. Add onion and garlic, and sauté for 3-4 minutes until softened.
4. Stir in kale and cook until wilted, about 2 minutes.
5. In a bowl, whisk together eggs, milk, salt, and pepper. Pour the mixture over the veggies in the skillet.
6. Cook over medium heat for 4-5 minutes until the edges begin to set.
7. Transfer the skillet to the oven and bake for 10-12 minutes until the center is set.
8. Garnish with feta cheese if desired and serve warm.

Baked Chicken Parmesan with Zoodles

Ingredients:

- 4 boneless, skinless chicken breasts
- 1 cup breadcrumbs (use gluten-free if needed)
- 1/4 cup grated Parmesan cheese
- 1 egg, beaten
- 1 cup marinara sauce
- 1 cup shredded mozzarella cheese
- 2 zucchinis, spiralized into noodles (zoodles)
- 1 tablespoon olive oil
- Salt and pepper to taste

Instructions:

1. Preheat the oven to 400°F (200°C).
2. In a shallow bowl, combine breadcrumbs, Parmesan, salt, and pepper.
3. Dip each chicken breast into the beaten egg, then coat with the breadcrumb mixture.
4. Place the chicken breasts on a baking sheet and bake for 20-25 minutes until golden and cooked through.
5. While the chicken bakes, heat olive oil in a pan and sauté zoodles for 2-3 minutes until tender. Season with salt and pepper.
6. Remove chicken from the oven, top with marinara sauce and mozzarella cheese, and return to the oven for an additional 5-7 minutes until the cheese is melted.
7. Serve the chicken over the zoodles and enjoy!

Veggie and Hummus Stuffed Pita

Ingredients:

- 4 whole wheat pita pockets
- 1/2 cup hummus
- 1 cucumber, thinly sliced
- 1 red bell pepper, sliced
- 1 small tomato, diced
- 1/4 red onion, thinly sliced
- 1/4 cup fresh parsley, chopped
- Salt and pepper to taste

Instructions:

1. Slice the pita pockets in half to create 4 pockets.
2. Spread a generous amount of hummus inside each pita.
3. Stuff the pita with cucumber, bell pepper, tomato, onion, and parsley.
4. Season with salt and pepper, then serve immediately for a light, healthy lunch or snack.

Spicy Black Bean and Avocado Salad

Ingredients:

- 1 can black beans, drained and rinsed
- 1 avocado, diced
- 1/2 red onion, finely chopped
- 1 red bell pepper, diced
- 1 jalapeño, finely chopped (optional for heat)
- 1 tablespoon lime juice
- 1 teaspoon olive oil
- 1/4 teaspoon cumin
- Salt and pepper to taste
- Fresh cilantro, chopped, for garnish

Instructions:

1. In a large bowl, combine black beans, avocado, onion, bell pepper, and jalapeño.
2. In a small bowl, whisk together lime juice, olive oil, cumin, salt, and pepper.
3. Pour the dressing over the salad and toss gently to combine.
4. Garnish with fresh cilantro and serve as a refreshing side dish or light meal.

Roasted Brussels Sprouts and Sweet Potato

Ingredients:

- 1 lb Brussels sprouts, trimmed and halved
- 2 medium sweet potatoes, peeled and diced
- 2 tablespoons olive oil
- 1 teaspoon dried thyme
- Salt and pepper to taste
- 1 tablespoon balsamic vinegar (optional)

Instructions:

1. Preheat the oven to 400°F (200°C).
2. Toss Brussels sprouts and sweet potatoes in olive oil, thyme, salt, and pepper.
3. Spread the vegetables on a baking sheet in a single layer.
4. Roast for 25-30 minutes, stirring halfway through, until vegetables are tender and golden.
5. Drizzle with balsamic vinegar if desired and serve warm.

Turkey and Spinach Meatloaf

Ingredients:

- 1 lb ground turkey
- 1 cup spinach, chopped
- 1/2 cup breadcrumbs (or almond flour for low-carb option)
- 1/4 cup grated Parmesan cheese
- 1 egg
- 1 tablespoon ketchup
- 1/2 teaspoon dried oregano
- Salt and pepper to taste
- 1/4 cup marinara sauce (for topping)

Instructions:

1. Preheat the oven to 375°F (190°C).
2. In a large bowl, combine ground turkey, spinach, breadcrumbs, Parmesan, egg, ketchup, oregano, salt, and pepper.
3. Transfer the mixture to a loaf pan and shape into a loaf.
4. Spread marinara sauce on top of the meatloaf.
5. Bake for 40-45 minutes until cooked through and golden on top.
6. Serve with steamed vegetables or a side salad.

Quinoa Salad with Roasted Vegetables

Ingredients:

- 1 cup quinoa, rinsed
- 1 tablespoon olive oil
- 1 cup diced sweet potatoes
- 1 cup zucchini, diced
- 1 cup cherry tomatoes, halved
- 1/4 cup feta cheese (optional)
- 2 tablespoons fresh parsley, chopped
- 1 tablespoon lemon juice
- Salt and pepper to taste

Instructions:

1. Preheat the oven to 400°F (200°C).
2. Toss sweet potatoes, zucchini, and tomatoes in olive oil, salt, and pepper. Roast for 20-25 minutes until tender.
3. Cook quinoa according to package instructions.
4. In a large bowl, combine quinoa, roasted vegetables, feta, parsley, and lemon juice.
5. Toss gently and serve warm or chilled.

Garlic Parmesan Roasted Shrimp

Ingredients:

- 1 lb large shrimp, peeled and deveined
- 2 tablespoons olive oil
- 4 garlic cloves, minced
- 1/4 teaspoon red pepper flakes (optional)
- 1/4 cup grated Parmesan cheese
- Salt and pepper to taste
- 1 tablespoon fresh parsley, chopped

Instructions:

1. Preheat the oven to 400°F (200°C).
2. Toss shrimp with olive oil, garlic, red pepper flakes, Parmesan, salt, and pepper.
3. Spread the shrimp in a single layer on a baking sheet.
4. Roast for 8-10 minutes, until shrimp are pink and cooked through.
5. Garnish with fresh parsley and serve immediately.

Broccoli and Cheddar Stuffed Chicken Breast

Ingredients:

- 4 boneless, skinless chicken breasts
- 1 cup broccoli florets, steamed and chopped
- 1/2 cup shredded cheddar cheese
- 2 tablespoons cream cheese (optional for creaminess)
- 1 tablespoon olive oil
- Salt and pepper to taste
- 1 teaspoon garlic powder

Instructions:

1. Preheat the oven to 375°F (190°C).
2. Cut a pocket into each chicken breast, being careful not to cut all the way through.
3. In a bowl, combine steamed broccoli, cheddar cheese, cream cheese, salt, and pepper.
4. Stuff the broccoli mixture into the pocket of each chicken breast.
5. Rub the chicken breasts with olive oil and sprinkle with garlic powder, salt, and pepper.
6. Place the stuffed chicken breasts on a baking sheet and bake for 25-30 minutes until the chicken is cooked through and the cheese is melted.
7. Serve warm and enjoy!

Grilled Chicken with Greek Salad

Ingredients:

- 4 boneless, skinless chicken breasts
- 2 tablespoons olive oil
- 1 teaspoon dried oregano
- Salt and pepper to taste
- 1 cucumber, diced
- 1 cup cherry tomatoes, halved
- 1/2 red onion, thinly sliced
- 1/2 cup Kalamata olives
- 1/4 cup crumbled feta cheese
- 2 tablespoons olive oil (for the salad dressing)
- 1 tablespoon red wine vinegar
- 1 teaspoon lemon juice
- 1 teaspoon dried oregano

Instructions:

1. Preheat the grill to medium-high heat.
2. Rub chicken breasts with olive oil, oregano, salt, and pepper.
3. Grill the chicken for 6-7 minutes per side until fully cooked and juices run clear.
4. While the chicken cooks, prepare the salad by combining cucumber, tomatoes, red onion, olives, and feta in a large bowl.
5. In a small bowl, whisk together olive oil, red wine vinegar, lemon juice, oregano, salt, and pepper to create the dressing.
6. Toss the salad with the dressing.
7. Serve the grilled chicken on a plate with a generous serving of the Greek salad.

Avocado and Tuna Salad Lettuce Wraps

Ingredients:

- 1 can tuna, drained
- 1 ripe avocado, diced
- 1 tablespoon mayonnaise or Greek yogurt
- 1 tablespoon lemon juice
- 1/4 teaspoon garlic powder
- Salt and pepper to taste
- 4 large lettuce leaves (butter or Romaine)
- Fresh cilantro, chopped (optional)

Instructions:

1. In a bowl, combine tuna, avocado, mayonnaise (or yogurt), lemon juice, garlic powder, salt, and pepper.
2. Mix until well combined.
3. Spoon the tuna mixture into the center of each lettuce leaf.
4. Garnish with fresh cilantro if desired.
5. Serve immediately as a light and refreshing lunch or snack.

Roasted Vegetables with Tahini Dressing

Ingredients:

- 1 cup carrots, sliced
- 1 cup cauliflower florets
- 1 cup Brussels sprouts, halved
- 2 tablespoons olive oil
- Salt and pepper to taste
- 1/4 cup tahini
- 2 tablespoons lemon juice
- 1 tablespoon water (or more for desired consistency)
- 1 clove garlic, minced
- 1 tablespoon maple syrup or honey (optional)

Instructions:

1. Preheat the oven to 400°F (200°C).
2. Toss carrots, cauliflower, and Brussels sprouts with olive oil, salt, and pepper.
3. Spread the vegetables on a baking sheet in a single layer and roast for 25-30 minutes, stirring halfway through, until tender and golden.
4. In a small bowl, whisk together tahini, lemon juice, water, garlic, and maple syrup (if using) until smooth.
5. Drizzle the tahini dressing over the roasted vegetables and serve warm.

Coconut Curry Chicken and Veggies

Ingredients:

- 1 lb chicken breast, cubed
- 2 tablespoons olive oil
- 1 onion, chopped
- 2 garlic cloves, minced
- 1 tablespoon ginger, grated
- 1 tablespoon curry powder
- 1 can coconut milk (full-fat)
- 1 cup bell peppers, diced
- 1 cup zucchini, diced
- Salt and pepper to taste
- Fresh cilantro, chopped (for garnish)

Instructions:

1. Heat olive oil in a large pan over medium heat. Add chicken and cook until browned on all sides, about 5-7 minutes.
2. Remove chicken from the pan and set aside.
3. In the same pan, add onion, garlic, and ginger. Sauté until the onion becomes soft and translucent.
4. Add curry powder and cook for 1-2 minutes, stirring constantly.
5. Pour in coconut milk and bring to a simmer. Add bell peppers and zucchini and cook for 5 minutes.
6. Return chicken to the pan and simmer for an additional 10-12 minutes until the chicken is cooked through.
7. Season with salt and pepper, garnish with cilantro, and serve with rice or quinoa.

Blackened Salmon with Quinoa

Ingredients:

- 4 salmon fillets
- 2 tablespoons olive oil
- 1 tablespoon paprika
- 1 teaspoon garlic powder
- 1 teaspoon onion powder
- 1/2 teaspoon cayenne pepper
- Salt and pepper to taste
- 1 cup quinoa, rinsed
- 2 cups water or chicken broth
- Lemon wedges for garnish

Instructions:

1. Preheat the oven to 375°F (190°C).
2. Mix paprika, garlic powder, onion powder, cayenne pepper, salt, and pepper in a small bowl.
3. Rub the spice mixture evenly over the salmon fillets.
4. Heat olive oil in a skillet over medium-high heat. Add salmon and cook for 3-4 minutes per side until the outside is blackened and the salmon is cooked through.
5. Meanwhile, cook quinoa by bringing water or broth to a boil. Reduce heat, cover, and simmer for 15 minutes or until quinoa is tender and fluffy.
6. Serve the blackened salmon over quinoa with lemon wedges.

Roasted Cauliflower with Tahini

Ingredients:

- 1 head cauliflower, cut into florets
- 2 tablespoons olive oil
- Salt and pepper to taste
- 1/4 cup tahini
- 2 tablespoons lemon juice
- 1 tablespoon water (or more for desired consistency)
- 1 garlic clove, minced
- Fresh parsley, chopped (for garnish)

Instructions:

1. Preheat the oven to 400°F (200°C).
2. Toss cauliflower florets in olive oil, salt, and pepper. Spread on a baking sheet.
3. Roast for 25-30 minutes, stirring halfway through, until golden and crispy on the edges.
4. In a small bowl, whisk together tahini, lemon juice, water, and garlic until smooth.
5. Drizzle the tahini dressing over the roasted cauliflower and garnish with parsley.

Sweet Potato and Spinach Gratin

Ingredients:

- 2 medium sweet potatoes, peeled and sliced thinly
- 2 cups spinach, chopped
- 1 cup heavy cream
- 1/2 cup grated Parmesan cheese
- 1/2 teaspoon garlic powder
- Salt and pepper to taste
- 1 tablespoon olive oil

Instructions:

1. Preheat the oven to 375°F (190°C).
2. Layer sliced sweet potatoes and spinach in a greased baking dish.
3. In a bowl, whisk together heavy cream, Parmesan, garlic powder, salt, and pepper.
4. Pour the cream mixture over the sweet potatoes and spinach.
5. Cover with foil and bake for 25 minutes. Remove the foil and bake for an additional 10-15 minutes until golden and tender.
6. Serve warm.

Grilled Portobello Mushrooms with Feta

Ingredients:

- 4 large Portobello mushroom caps, cleaned and stems removed
- 2 tablespoons olive oil
- 1 teaspoon balsamic vinegar
- 1 teaspoon garlic powder
- 1/2 teaspoon dried thyme
- Salt and pepper to taste
- 1/4 cup crumbled feta cheese
- Fresh parsley, chopped (for garnish)

Instructions:

1. Preheat the grill to medium heat.
2. Brush mushroom caps with olive oil, balsamic vinegar, garlic powder, thyme, salt, and pepper.
3. Grill mushrooms for 5-7 minutes per side until tender.
4. Sprinkle with feta cheese and garnish with parsley before serving.

Miso Glazed Chicken with Veggies

Ingredients:

- 4 boneless, skinless chicken breasts
- 2 tablespoons miso paste
- 1 tablespoon soy sauce
- 1 tablespoon honey
- 1 tablespoon rice vinegar
- 1 teaspoon sesame oil
- 2 cups mixed vegetables (broccoli, carrots, bell peppers)
- 1 tablespoon olive oil

Instructions:

1. Preheat the oven to 375°F (190°C).
2. In a small bowl, whisk together miso paste, soy sauce, honey, rice vinegar, and sesame oil.
3. Brush chicken breasts with the miso glaze and bake for 25-30 minutes until the chicken is cooked through.
4. Meanwhile, toss mixed vegetables with olive oil, salt, and pepper. Roast in the oven for 20 minutes or until tender.
5. Serve the glazed chicken with roasted veggies.

Tempeh and Vegetable Stir-Fry

Ingredients:

- 1 block tempeh, sliced into thin strips
- 1 tablespoon sesame oil
- 1 onion, thinly sliced
- 1 bell pepper, sliced
- 1 zucchini, sliced
- 1 cup broccoli florets
- 2 cloves garlic, minced
- 2 tablespoons soy sauce (or tamari for gluten-free)
- 1 tablespoon rice vinegar
- 1 tablespoon honey or maple syrup
- 1 teaspoon grated ginger
- 1 tablespoon sesame seeds (optional)
- Fresh cilantro for garnish (optional)

Instructions:

1. Heat sesame oil in a large skillet or wok over medium heat.
2. Add the tempeh strips and cook until golden and slightly crispy, about 5-7 minutes. Remove and set aside.
3. In the same pan, add onion, bell pepper, zucchini, and broccoli. Stir-fry for 5-7 minutes until the vegetables are tender-crisp.
4. Add garlic and ginger, cooking for 1 minute until fragrant.
5. Stir in soy sauce, rice vinegar, and honey/maple syrup. Return the tempeh to the pan and toss everything together.
6. Cook for another 2-3 minutes to combine the flavors. Sprinkle with sesame seeds and garnish with fresh cilantro before serving.

Greek Chicken Souvlaki Bowls

Ingredients:

- 4 boneless, skinless chicken breasts
- 2 tablespoons olive oil
- 2 tablespoons lemon juice
- 2 teaspoons dried oregano
- 1 teaspoon garlic powder
- Salt and pepper to taste
- 1 cup cooked quinoa or brown rice
- 1 cucumber, diced
- 1 cup cherry tomatoes, halved
- 1/2 red onion, thinly sliced
- 1/4 cup Kalamata olives, sliced
- 1/4 cup crumbled feta cheese
- Tzatziki sauce for drizzling (store-bought or homemade)

Instructions:

1. In a bowl, combine olive oil, lemon juice, oregano, garlic powder, salt, and pepper. Marinate the chicken breasts in the mixture for at least 30 minutes.
2. Preheat a grill or grill pan over medium-high heat. Grill chicken for 6-7 minutes per side until fully cooked and juices run clear.
3. While the chicken cooks, prepare the bowls by layering cooked quinoa or rice, cucumber, tomatoes, red onion, olives, and feta.
4. Slice the grilled chicken and arrange it on top of the vegetables and grains.
5. Drizzle with tzatziki sauce and serve immediately.

Roasted Eggplant with Tomato Sauce

Ingredients:

- 2 medium eggplants, sliced into 1/2-inch thick rounds
- 2 tablespoons olive oil
- Salt and pepper to taste
- 1 cup marinara sauce (store-bought or homemade)
- 1/4 cup fresh basil, chopped
- 1/4 cup grated Parmesan cheese (optional)

Instructions:

1. Preheat the oven to 400°F (200°C). Line a baking sheet with parchment paper.
2. Brush eggplant slices with olive oil and season with salt and pepper. Arrange in a single layer on the prepared baking sheet.
3. Roast for 25-30 minutes, flipping halfway through, until the eggplant is tender and golden.
4. In a small saucepan, heat marinara sauce over low heat.
5. To serve, top each eggplant slice with a spoonful of tomato sauce, a sprinkle of fresh basil, and Parmesan cheese if using. Serve warm.

Zucchini and Carrot Fritters

Ingredients:

- 2 medium zucchinis, grated
- 2 medium carrots, grated
- 2 eggs
- 1/2 cup almond flour (or all-purpose flour)
- 1/4 teaspoon garlic powder
- 1/4 teaspoon onion powder
- Salt and pepper to taste
- 2 tablespoons olive oil (for frying)
- Fresh parsley for garnish (optional)

Instructions:

1. Place grated zucchini and carrots in a clean kitchen towel or cheesecloth and squeeze out excess moisture.
2. In a large bowl, combine grated zucchini, carrots, eggs, almond flour, garlic powder, onion powder, salt, and pepper. Mix well to form a batter.
3. Heat olive oil in a skillet over medium heat. Drop spoonfuls of the batter into the pan and flatten slightly with the back of the spoon.
4. Fry for 3-4 minutes per side until golden and crispy.
5. Transfer the fritters to a paper towel-lined plate to drain excess oil. Garnish with fresh parsley before serving.

Grilled Cod with Cucumber Salad

Ingredients:

- 4 cod fillets
- 2 tablespoons olive oil
- 1 teaspoon lemon zest
- Salt and pepper to taste
- 1 cucumber, thinly sliced
- 1/4 cup red onion, thinly sliced
- 1 tablespoon fresh dill, chopped
- 1 tablespoon lemon juice
- 1 tablespoon olive oil (for salad)

Instructions:

1. Preheat the grill to medium-high heat.
2. Brush cod fillets with olive oil, lemon zest, salt, and pepper.
3. Grill cod for 4-5 minutes per side, or until the fish flakes easily with a fork.
4. While the fish cooks, prepare the cucumber salad by combining cucumber, red onion, dill, lemon juice, and olive oil in a bowl. Toss to combine.
5. Serve the grilled cod on a plate with the cucumber salad on the side. Garnish with additional fresh dill if desired.

Tofu and Broccoli Stir-Fry

Ingredients:

- 1 block firm tofu, drained and cubed
- 2 tablespoons soy sauce (or tamari for gluten-free)
- 1 tablespoon sesame oil
- 2 cloves garlic, minced
- 1 tablespoon fresh ginger, grated
- 1 cup broccoli florets
- 1 bell pepper, sliced
- 1/2 onion, sliced
- 1 tablespoon rice vinegar
- 1 tablespoon honey or maple syrup
- 1 tablespoon sesame seeds (optional)
- Fresh cilantro for garnish (optional)

Instructions:

1. Heat sesame oil in a large skillet or wok over medium heat. Add the tofu cubes and cook until golden brown on all sides, about 5-7 minutes. Remove tofu and set aside.
2. In the same pan, add garlic and ginger, cooking for 1 minute until fragrant.
3. Add broccoli, bell pepper, and onion. Stir-fry for 5-7 minutes, until vegetables are tender-crisp.
4. Stir in soy sauce, rice vinegar, and honey/maple syrup. Add tofu back to the pan and toss everything together to combine.
5. Cook for another 2-3 minutes. Garnish with sesame seeds and fresh cilantro before serving.

Coconut Lime Chicken with Rice

Ingredients:

- 4 boneless, skinless chicken breasts
- 1 can (13.5 oz) coconut milk
- 1 tablespoon lime zest
- 2 tablespoons lime juice
- 1 teaspoon garlic powder
- Salt and pepper to taste
- 1 cup cooked white or brown rice
- Fresh cilantro for garnish (optional)

Instructions:

1. In a bowl, combine coconut milk, lime zest, lime juice, garlic powder, salt, and pepper. Place chicken breasts in a shallow dish and pour the marinade over them. Marinate for at least 30 minutes.
2. Preheat a grill or skillet over medium heat. Cook chicken for 6-7 minutes per side, or until fully cooked and juices run clear.
3. While the chicken cooks, prepare the rice according to package instructions.
4. Serve the chicken over the cooked rice, drizzling with any remaining coconut-lime sauce. Garnish with fresh cilantro if desired.

Beetroot Salad with Walnuts

Ingredients:

- 2 medium beets, peeled and thinly sliced
- 1/2 cup walnuts, toasted
- 1 tablespoon olive oil
- 1 tablespoon balsamic vinegar
- 1 teaspoon honey or maple syrup
- Salt and pepper to taste
- 1/4 cup crumbled feta cheese (optional)
- Fresh parsley for garnish (optional)

Instructions:

1. Preheat the oven to 375°F (190°C). Wrap the beets in aluminum foil and roast for 45-60 minutes until tender. Allow them to cool, then peel and slice.
2. In a small bowl, whisk together olive oil, balsamic vinegar, honey/maple syrup, salt, and pepper.
3. In a large bowl, combine the roasted beets, toasted walnuts, and feta cheese (if using). Drizzle with the dressing and toss gently.
4. Garnish with fresh parsley before serving.

Mediterranean Chickpea Salad

Ingredients:

- 1 can (15 oz) chickpeas, drained and rinsed
- 1 cucumber, diced
- 1 cup cherry tomatoes, halved
- 1/4 red onion, finely chopped
- 1/4 cup Kalamata olives, sliced
- 1/4 cup crumbled feta cheese
- 1 tablespoon olive oil
- 1 tablespoon lemon juice
- 1 teaspoon dried oregano
- Salt and pepper to taste

Instructions:

1. In a large bowl, combine chickpeas, cucumber, tomatoes, red onion, olives, and feta.
2. In a small bowl, whisk together olive oil, lemon juice, oregano, salt, and pepper.
3. Pour the dressing over the salad and toss gently to combine. Serve chilled or at room temperature.

Quinoa and Black Bean Stuffed Peppers

Ingredients:

- 4 bell peppers, tops cut off and seeds removed
- 1 cup cooked quinoa
- 1 can (15 oz) black beans, drained and rinsed
- 1 cup corn kernels (fresh, frozen, or canned)
- 1 teaspoon cumin
- 1 teaspoon chili powder
- Salt and pepper to taste
- 1/4 cup shredded cheese (optional)
- Fresh cilantro for garnish (optional)

Instructions:

1. Preheat the oven to 375°F (190°C). Place the bell peppers in a baking dish.
2. In a bowl, combine cooked quinoa, black beans, corn, cumin, chili powder, salt, and pepper.
3. Stuff the mixture into the bell peppers and top with cheese (if using).
4. Cover the baking dish with foil and bake for 25-30 minutes, until the peppers are tender.
5. Garnish with fresh cilantro before serving.

Grilled Veggie and Quinoa Bowl

Ingredients:

- 1 cup cooked quinoa
- 1 zucchini, sliced
- 1 red bell pepper, sliced
- 1 small eggplant, sliced
- 1 tablespoon olive oil
- Salt and pepper to taste
- 1 tablespoon balsamic vinegar
- 1 tablespoon tahini (optional)
- Fresh basil for garnish (optional)

Instructions:

1. Preheat the grill or grill pan to medium-high heat. Brush the vegetables with olive oil and season with salt and pepper.
2. Grill the zucchini, bell pepper, and eggplant for 3-4 minutes per side until tender and slightly charred.
3. In a bowl, combine the cooked quinoa and grilled vegetables. Drizzle with balsamic vinegar and tahini (if using).
4. Toss everything together and garnish with fresh basil before serving.

www.ingramcontent.com/pod-product-compliance
Lightning Source LLC
LaVergne TN
LVHW081338060526
838201LV00055B/2724